CW01018823

One Tooth Luce

& Other Stories

Luce Watson

Cover by: Ellie Hulme

For my grandma, Margaret

"If my life wasn't funny it would just be true, and that is unacceptable."

Carrie Fisher

ACKNOWLEDGMENTS

A special thanks to Ellie Hulme for bringing One Tooth Luce to life with her visual creativity. Thank you to Poppy Hudghton and Amy Billington for checking that everything I write makes sense. Thank you to Emily Sutton and Becca McKeown for helping me on the night I lost my tooth. And to Charlotte Fowler for staying calm when I broke my ankle. Thank you to my parents for putting up with me and making me nice food.

Most importantly, thank you to Nick, Joe and Kevin, without whom, this book would not exist.

INTRODUCTION

I've not had the greatest of years. Nor has anyone, really. I promised myself that I wouldn't make this book about the Coronavirus disease (Covid-19) 2020 pandemic because I don't want to give it the satisfaction or attention. But I think I speak for everyone when I say SARS-CoV-2, go fuck yourself.

Besides all of the major global disasters, my year has been particularly shit. It has been one of those years where every bad thing that you could ever possibly imagine happening in your life, happens. Where you think, "oh that'll never happen to me", and then it does. Many times.

If you're here it might be because I blackmailed you into reading this book, in which case, welcome! Or it might be because you've also had a shite year and you want to feel better about yourself, in which case, hello! Or maybe this hasn't been published and you're my dad and I'm making you read this to check for grammatical errors, in which case, be nice!

Whoever you are, I hope these chapters entertain/inspire/educate you into realising you're not alone in being an absolute fucking mess, even if it looks like you're thriving.

First of all, I'm not thriving. As I'm writing this it's one of those unbelievably warm nights in the middle of November when all I want to do is take all of my clothes off but I can't because I'm worried someone might hack my laptop camera and take pictures and post them all over the internet.

I'm a twenty-seven year old with two purple scars on my left leg and no front tooth. I'm also unemployed and I live with my parents. Good. Now that we've got all of that out of the way we can all relax. You're not thriving either? Amazing. Welcome to the club. Let's all take a long, deep breath. There's something very comforting about realising you're not alone.

I remember turning up to my mate's flat on New Year's Eve with the optimism that 2020 was going to be my year. I'd had a terrible 2019 that ended in a painfully tragic break up and a few mental hurdles (mostly spurred on by the painfully tragic break up), and I was ready to start on a clean slate. I'm not even kidding about the part where I believed 2020 was going to be my year. I really, really believed it.

At the end of 2019, I envisaged a future full of holidays and happiness and a big, fat salary. Instead, I received mandatory lockdown, depression and a big, fat lip.

Anyone who knows me will tell you I'm a glass half full kind of person. I mean, most of the time I'm annoyingly positive, which might have something to do with the medication I'm on, and the rest of the time I'm an anxious mess. But even when I'm an anxious mess, I like all of my glasses to be half full and not half empty. Unless you're offering me wine, in which case make it full full.

So I guess my point is, this book is my way of taking this year full of shite and turning it into something positive, like an entertaining year full of shite.

Disclaimer: not all of my 2020 has been shite. Some of it has actually been very good. But very good doesn't make for funny stories. Sorry.

I hope this confusing introduction hasn't put you off. If it has, this book gets gory, I promise.

ONE TOOTH LUCE

I lost my front tooth on February 6th 2020 after a Jonas Brothers concert. Yes I know, how unbelievable: the Jonas Brothers are still a thing.

Before I start the whole tooth saga I need to say for my barely intact reputation that I've not always been clumsy. I mean there was that one time at a funeral when I knocked over a buffet table; and the time I spilt a glass of wine all over my date. And also that time I rolled a bowling ball backwards instead of forwards. But aside from those extremely isolated incidents, my ability to remain confidently planted on two feet was pretty stellar. Fine. I'm lying. But massage my ego and tell me I had you going for a second.

My friend Emily works in Public Relations and managed to get us free tickets to the Jonas Brothers concert in Manchester. Like most people born in the early 1990s, I was a teen raised on the Disney Channel and I grew up thinking *Camp Rock* was a real place, so obviously, I was going to go and I would be lying if I said I wasn't excited. (I probably did lie and tell a few people I wasn't excited).

Fourteen-year-old Lucy would fantasise about marrying Nick Jonas. I believed with all my heart that this union was going to happen. I was convinced that we'd meet one day, by chance, and he would fall head over heels in love.

This infatuation was only intensified when Nick Jonas made eye contact with me at their concert in 2009. Important context: I'm a Pisces. Six days out of seven I live in a dreamy land. More important context: I'm gay now. But fortunately, my love for Nick Jonas defies labels.

Emily and I arrived at the arena and went straight to the bar. We ordered a bottle of white wine that could only be described as a heart burner and found our seats.

Feeling sociable, I turned to the girls next to me and asked how long they'd been fans of the Jonas Brothers.

"Since I was like thirteen," one of them said.

"No way, me too," I replied.

Turns out they were seventeen. Feeling ancient, we ordered more wine.

Emily and I danced, drank, sang, drank, screamed, drank some more. The atmosphere was electric and we were two women in our late twenties acting like teenagers again.

I remembered what it felt like to be obsessed with someone completely unobtainable. "I'm going to marry Nick Jonas," I announced.

"I'm going to marry Joe!" In our drunken state, anything was possible.

When the set finished, we agreed that it was probably the best concert we'd ever been to but we shouldn't, under any circumstances, tell anyone else that.

Into the fresh air and teenaged crowds, Emily and I decided it was a good idea to meet our friend Becca for more drinks. After all, we were both newly engaged to a Jonas sibling and we needed to celebrate the occasion.

If you've ever been friends with someone who works in PR, you'll know it usually means connections in all the best bars, free shit and nights that never end. Best case scenario was waking up in the canal the next morning with a mouth like sandpaper and a missing shoe.

Emily ordered a taxi and we waited outside the arena acting as though we were completely sober.

It was obvious we weren't because Emily was doing that thing drunk people do when they're on their phones and they sway from side to side like they're on a boat. After a few minutes, our driver messaged to say he was stuck in traffic. He was going to wait and we needed to walk to him. It seemed like an easy enough task but a bit lazy on his part if you ask me.

Off we went. I slipped my hands into my pockets, put one foot in front of the other, and hit the pavement with my face. What's that you ask? Why didn't I put my hands out to break my fall? My only response is I don't know why I didn't put my hands out to break my fall. That would've been a very smart idea and would've saved my grandparents thousands of pounds.

Completely dazed, I sat up and touched the front of my mouth with my tongue. Emily's eyes widened in horror. My right front tooth was gone and half of my left tooth was chipped.

The best part is this isn't the first time I've chipped my front teeth. The first time was when I was in year nine P.E. and we had to hop across the sports hall wearing blindfolds. So, of course, I jumped face-first into a brick wall. Health and safety? Never heard of her. We didn't end up suing the school and it's one of my mum's biggest regrets to this day.

Emily dropped to her knees, instantly sobered, and shoved her cardigan in my mouth to stop the bleeding. It felt like a giant ball of cotton wool against my gums.

"I've lost my front tooth..." I screamed into the cardigan.

"Lucy, it's going to be OK."

The PR in her took over. While I wailed all over the floor, she knew exactly what to do. She phoned Becca. She contacted my parents and my sister. She called the taxi driver and told him we had a change of plan. Emily was my hero that night and I'll never be able to thank her for everything she did.

After a short while, Becca appeared, out of breath. You know when you have an accident and your friends pretend it's fine like you haven't completely fucked up your face? Yeah, that happened.

I cried into Emily's cardigan as Becca looked for my missing tooth on her hands and knees. What we must've looked like to passersby doesn't even bear thinking about.

We entered A&E to a room full of people with actual injuries. You know, ones sustained in car crashes and alike. I, the girl who had knocked her front tooth out after face-planting the pavement, felt like a fraud as I walked up to the receptionist with my cut-up fat lip. She took one look at me and told me to sit down while Becca and Emily gave her my information.

My family arrived not long after and assessed the damage. My favourite suit was covered in blood and my make-up was smudged down my cheeks. My mum and sister took me into the toilet and tried to clean me up. I was drunk and in shock, and all I said over and over again was, "I've lost my fucking front tooth."

I stumbled out of the bathroom and announced to the waiting room full of invalids that I'd lost my fucking front tooth. To my shock and disappointment, nobody cared.

We sat in the hospital for hours, most of the time in silence. Feeling pangs of despair at how shite my 2020 was going so far, I did what all insecure millennials do and went on my dating app messages. I'd matched with a girl that night and after everything that had happened I was feeling brave, so I asked if I could buy her a Greggs and a drink. She replied instantly and said yes. I had no front tooth, a fat lip, and the self-esteem of a melon, but she said yes.

I had three x-rays to check that a) I hadn't swallowed my tooth, b) my tooth wasn't lodged in my lip, and c) there was no tooth left in my gum. I hadn't; it wasn't; there wasn't. At this point I should've been happy that my missing tooth wasn't floating aimlessly in my body but I wasn't. I wanted them to find it because a naive part of me hoped it was possible for them to shove it back in there like nothing had happened. Instead it's probably hanging on a chain around some Mancunian's neck.

We got home just after four in the morning and I felt like I'd lived an entire year in the space of one night. I was in incredible pain. The former tooth site and entire mouth/chin region was on fire and throbbing, and not in a good sexy way. And if that wasn't enough, resting my oozing face against a white pillow was already setting me up to fail.

Tooth, wherever you are, I miss you. I hope you're doing well.

TWO

In the mirror the next morning, I was a pig. Self-deprecating humour is my speciality but in this instance, it was just accurate information.

My face had swollen dramatically overnight which meant, in comparison, my eyes resembled sad little blueberries. I had a trout pout that would deter any one of the Kardashians from getting more plastic surgery and when I opened my mouth, it might as well have been a crime scene.

When you lose a tooth, anyone, and I mean *anyone*, who has ever experienced something similar comes crawling out of the woodwork with a story: a friend's auntie; a next-door neighbour; your grandma's friend's dog.

I heard several anecdotes over the following couple of weeks about losing teeth that made me feel hopeless and entertained all the same time. Stories that usually involved the toothless individual hiding away until their problem was fixed.

A big part of my hopelessness was to do with the price tag that came with securing a new tooth. I had 30p in my bank account, a benefits payment from the government every month, and a job promoting takeaway discounts on the streets in town. I couldn't afford an implant (a fake tooth that screws into your jaw), which was looking to cost the best part of three grand.

"Don't worry about it," Mum said. "We'll work something out." That was her way of saying she'd ask my dad very nicely and he'd ask my grandparents very nicely.

In secondary school I was bullied for the way I looked. It started in year seven and carried on until the day I left in 2009. I was shy, chubby and an easy target. It was incredibly fun and every night I go to bed and pray I will wake up as twelve-year-old me again.

The first time I lost my front teeth, I dreaded having to go back to school looking like I'd given a blow job to a steel rod. I was terrified of what people would say. More importantly, what my tormentors would say. I couldn't get fillings for two weeks, which meant I had to face the wrath of mean teens for ten whole days. I thought it was the worst thing that had ever happened to anyone ever ever ever and I spent most of my time at home sulking in my room, arms crossed and eyebrows furrowed.

The truth is that back then nobody cared about my toothlessness other than me. Nothing bad happened and nobody said anything. I was so concerned about what others thought that I forgot everyone else was doing exactly the same thing.

Imagine a group of people where each individual is so preoccupied with themselves that they don't pay any attention to that spot you've been trying to hide on your chin, or the dark circles under your eyes that you're so desperately self-conscious about. Would you still care what they thought?

I will say this: in 2020 my toothlessness has seen almost celebrity status. Everyone knew about my missing tooth because I did the narcissistic thing and posted it all over social media.

I did this for a couple of reasons: 1) because I thought it would be entertaining and make people laugh and 2) because I thought if people saw me getting on with my life sans front tooth, it might inspire them to care less about the smaller things that were bothering them. So I branded my journey and gave myself a nickname: One Tooth Luce.

It's very self-explanatory but if you're struggling: 'One Tooth' because I was missing one tooth and 'Luce' because that's my name. Also, my mum likes to point out that it's twice as clever because Luce is a homophone of 'loose' and that sort of fits with the whole missing tooth thing, aaanddd nobody cares. Sorry mum.

One Tooth Luce has become a version of myself that I'm incredibly proud of. She represents the aspect of my personality that doesn't give a fuck. And I'm surprised by how much I didn't give a fuck about missing a tooth.

My dentist confirmed it would be a few weeks until I'd have a temporary tooth lodged in there; I had a moment of panic, took a deep breath, and remembered it could be a lot worse. This thing wasn't going away quickly, so I needed to do what I did best and make it a joke.

THREE

Like anyone born in the early nineties, the first thing I did was make a new Instagram account; post a picture of my bloody mouth and missing teeth: "hi everyone (0 followers) I'm planning on milking this lost tooth saga for all its worth. Pls share this magical journey to a full set of teeth with me xox One Tooth Luce".

Turns out people were wildly entertained. Huh. Yes, the rumours were all true! Luce was funny!

I know funny people have the reputation of being the ugly ones in their friendship groups but in my case, it was tragically true. My school friends were statues with slender figures and perfect hair, and I looked like a round teen boy with hunched shoulders. I needed to be funny. I held onto it as desperately as I could, pushing out joke after joke until I heard laughter. I got a thrill out of making people laugh and I still do.

So here's the thing: having a missing tooth didn't bother me as much as I thought it would. It didn't really bother me at all. I couldn't say words like "soup" or "anaesthetic" without spitting in someone's eye but this was only to the amusement of my family and friends. My sister Grace would taunt me with words she knew I wouldn't be able to pronounce without it raining saliva. It was the most I'd laughed in months and all it took was eating concrete.

Now I'm not recommending knocking out your front tooth just to feel something, or to get people to like you. That would be terrible advice. But what I am endorsing is trying to find the positive in negative situations. It's not always easy and it will take some work but once you stop giving a fuck about what other people think of you, you realise there is so much fun to be had, even without a front tooth.

When I lost my tooth I made an effort not to hide-away. Dared myself to carry on as normal. After all, what was the worst that could happen other than a few stares?

The dentist was making a denture (£260?!) for me to wear temporarily until I got a permanent implant (£3,000?!?!) but I'd have to go toothless until then. Yes, a denture is what old people wear and yes, it is just as uncomfortable as it sounds. It looks like a pink plastic spider web with a fake tooth attached to it and you have to stick it in with special glue so it doesn't fall out. I wish I was joking. There are even different shades of fake tooth colours to choose from. I asked if mine could be hot pink and I was very upset when the answer was a resounding no.

I had a ticket for a gig in Manchester and I'd made up my mind I was going. The girl I'd been messaging asked for a photo of my mouth and I sent her the goriest one I could find, hoping she was just as disgusting as I was. Millennial dating is strange enough in normal situations but this was the first time I'd ever been asked to send a picture of my teeth. She replied instantly, impressed.

I turned to my friends in the back seat of the taxi. "She likes it."

"See, maybe losing a tooth was a good thing."

The night ended on Canal Street and I was surrounded by dancing gays asking what had happened to my face. I was out with my best friend Jamie and his boyfriend Tom and they were impressed by all of the male attention I was getting. I, a gay woman, was not.

We downed cheap vodka and danced to Robyn and took loads of pictures. It's like my fucked up face hadn't made any difference to our enjoyment and, oh wait! Why should it? Nobody cared. Nobody pointed and laughed. Nobody huddled together and whispered. Most importantly, we had fun.

FOUR

By February 14th, it was time to meet new people. I've always been single on Valentine's Day and 2020 was no different.

I'd been invited to tag along to my mate Amy's anti-Valentine's Day drinks in town, and the girl I was messaging texted to say she was going to be around too.

Despite the success of my previous night out, the prospect of meeting new people without a front tooth was still incredibly daunting.

"You're more than your tooth," my friend Poppy texted as I was on the train into town. She was right. It was a weak moment and I had failed at the first hurdle as One Tooth Luce. If I was going to enjoy myself, I'd have to embrace the toothless look, one hundred percent.

By this point my face was back to its regular shape (still round but just a bit less round) and the cut on my lip had healed. I was a bit disappointed that during the shrinking process it had conveniently left my double chin but I suppose you can't have everything.

At the bar, I started talking to a couple of guys and it wasn't long before the conversation turned to my missing tooth.

"How did it happen?"

"I tripped after seeing the Jonas Brothers."

"Are you being serious? I can't tell."

"Why would I joke about that? Surely I'd come up with a better story."

One of the lads cocked his head. "You know if you turn your face to the right you look completely normal."

Amy's friends arrived and joined us at the table. I was already two double vodkas in and was feeling a lot less nervous than two hours ago Luce. What was left of my other front tooth was agony every time I sipped my drink but I figured the drunker I got, the less I would be in pain. Science!

I was five months fresh out of a break up, which meant I fancied everyone and everything. I'd had a few unsuccessful first dates with various women (and one man) but back then I had all teeth accounted for and now kissing would involve the other person sticking their tongue through my gap. And here was my dilemma: I fancied one of Amy's mates.

It was one of those rare occasions when you meet another queer person in the wild and not on a dating app. Manchester is a relatively big city but the lesbian community is not. There's a chance that every gay woman in the city centre and surrounding has either kissed or shagged. Or at the very least, gone on a date.

Amy's friend was cool and nice, and after talking for a while it turned out we had a lot in common. So when I drunkenly suggested we have a snog in the toilets, I wasn't too surprised when she said yes. What did surprise me was that she said yes despite the gaping hole in the front of my mouth.

I asked her why she kissed me and her response was because I was confident. Huh. How many times have you thought you weren't good enough for someone because there was something about your appearance that you didn't like?

This was the moment all my insecurities about the way I looked, that I'd been holding onto for so many years, felt tremendously stupid. I'd just snogged a hot girl and she didn't care about my missing tooth. What had I been worrying about all this time?

So I'm drunk and having a good time, and the girl I'd been

messaging texted to say she wanted to meet. At this point, it was past midnight and we'd lost a couple from our group, and I was feeling pretty good about myself following my steamy exchange in the toilets. So fuck it. I texted her my location.

Here's the thing about alcohol: it makes you forget very exciting things that happen to you, such as meeting up with a beautiful, intelligent and interesting woman on a night out who you really fancy and have been nervous to meet because you have no tooth. So I'll do my best to fill in the blanks.

We exchanged pleasantries, sat down with our drinks and then proceeded to kiss each other rather aggressively in front of everyone in the bar. Kiss. Each other. With no tooth. Did I mention I had no front tooth?

Word of advice: the good ones won't care.

FIVE

I broke my ankle on August 13th 2020 after falling off a skateboard. I know what you're thinking: following the tooth incident, why didn't my mother wrap me in bubble wrap and lock me in my room?

At this point, I had a denture and we'd become very close and his name was Dennis. I'd also had a screw drilled into my gum ready for my permanent tooth, which was delayed due to the pandemic.

During the Covid-19 lockdown, skateboarding became my new hobby. I was bored out of my mind and thought it was time to try something new. My old fifteen quid skateboard was exactly where I left it in the garage and was home to at least three spider's nests. It was wobbly but fitted my extremely low criteria of a piece of wood with wheels, so I dusted it off and started practising in my kitchen.

I'd wanted to skate ever since I'd played the Tony Hawk video games on my PlayStation 2 when I was twelve. But here's the thing: I'd never been brave enough to skateboard because I was a girl and it's a very well known fact that teen girls do exactly what teen girls are supposed to do, which is stay away from footballs, or rugby balls, or skateboards, or BMXs, or anything that boys like to do.

It sounds incredibly stupid now because girls can obviously do anything boys can do, and more. But back then I was an insecure teenager and I didn't want to do anything to draw attention to myself.

When I was more confident, I started skating on the street outside my house. I was wobbling all over the place but I could balance, just about, and with each push I got better. And then a couple of months in, I fell off and did the splits and tore my hamstring.

Now I'm not very flexible and I've never done the splits in my life, accidentally or on purpose. It felt just as uncomfortable as I thought it would and anyone who can do the splits intentionally is a freak. I stand by that.

I knew I'd done something serious when I felt my leg *pop*. Nothing good ever comes from a noise like that, especially when body parts are involved. I limped to the house, made it into the kitchen and threw up all over the floor. And I mean projectile vomited, like a hose filling a paddling pool.

My parents stood at the end of the kitchen in shock. "What's going on?" Dad yelled, staring at my paddling pool of sick.

I was in agony and I was seeing stars, and mum forced my head down between my legs. Apparently, it's supposed to help but I just felt a bit daft making eye contact with my vomit. Dad made me sweet tea and I ate half a bar of chocolate. Not a regular sized one either. You know giant ones you get as a novelty at Christmas that are the size of a brick?

My leg was bad. Really really bad. So bad that I couldn't stand up. There was something seriously wrong down there. It felt like my muscles had collapsed. Like someone had taken a pair of scissors to my tightly wound guitar string tendons and hacked away.

My (very sensible) friends told me I should go to A&E but I (not very sensibly) refused. Instead, I lay on a sun lounger in the garden and took loads of painkillers, proud of my first skating injury. I know. I'm a terrible person.

FOOT LUCE

Four weeks later, I was healed and hobbling. Any sensible person would take this horrifying injury as a sign to stop skateboarding. Did I do that? Of course not.

A natural progression for any first-time skater is to go from street to skatepark because then you feel like the real thing. My best friend Charlotte and I had chosen the women's only night because it sounded less daunting and because we were both women, so already we were winning.

So we're skating, right? We're doing things that make us look cool, like roll up and down ramps and go at speeds greater than 3mph. We even have one-on-one coaching from a blonde girl called Connie. When she skated out it was that stomach-dropping moment when the person in front of you is incredibly hot and also a good skater and you just want to kill yourself.

Connie cheered me on as I psyched myself up to skate down a ramp that went up to my shin while I pretended not to be a nervous gay around her. Charlotte was a natural skater, as it turned out, and spent most of the evening out-skating me despite my three-month head start.

I should have a cooler story for what happened next but unfortunately, I don't. I considered lying by saying that I was in the middle of a 360 tail slide frontside fakie indie backflip but I can't glamourise it any more than I already have to my family and friends.

So here it is. The truth: I was riding towards my new skater gal pals feeling like 2001 Avril Lavigne and my board slipped from underneath me. But instead of my foot doing the normal foot thing and landing on my sole, it popped to the left and my ankle bone came out.

To recap: I was riding on flat ground, fell off my skateboard, and dislocated my ankle.

Everyone rushed over while I tried to stop myself from passing out. "I think it's broken," I said. "I think I'm going to faint."

"Take deep breaths," Charlotte said, making a pile of bags to rest my foot on.

I'd never broken a bone before so I didn't know how it was supposed to feel. My only experience was when my sister got run over in an ASDA car park and broke her ankle. My dad described Grace's blood-curdling scream in his ear as he talked to her best friend on the phone. Where was my blood-curdling scream? I didn't really feel anything. Was that normal?

I don't remember a lot of what happened next, just that there was a lot of panic and heavy breathing and a bit of laughter (?) and some Coca Cola. I was wrapped in a foil blanket so I didn't get cold (I still got cold) and Connie said an ambulance was on its way.

It is a testament to my parents that they haven't disowned me. I often look at my younger sister and wonder how she managed to come out so sensible, with her steady job and savings and lack of missing body parts. I also often wonder if my parents ever see me as the fuck up. When I phoned my mum and told her I'd fallen off my skateboard and broken my ankle I heard a disappointing sigh. In a year already tarred with personal disasters my broken ankle was just another thing for my parents to worry about.

The ambulance arrived once the skate park had closed and the paramedics were two jolly middle-aged men called Steve and Paul. Paul, grey-haired with a dad-bod, tapped several spots on my foot to check my circulation levels and then marked the top with an X. Apparently this was a good thing and meant I could keep my foot. Phew. We'd become good friends.

Steve and Paul helped me onto the stretcher and strapped me in like a sardine, and then wheeled me up and down the quarter pipes as we exited the park. I laughed like a toddler with her two gay dads, and then I asked them if they could take a picture.

Paul turned his back and Steve took my phone. "We could get in trouble for this but because it's on your phone…" Ambulance Police if you're reading this, I coerced Steve and Paul into taking a photo. I'm a bad person. Poor Steve and Paul didn't have a choice.

It turns out my ankle was broken in three places and bits were hanging off that shouldn't have been hanging off. My fibula (the thin leg bone) had snapped in half and my tibia (the fat leg bone) had two chunks missing.

I cried my eyes out and being the drama queen that I am, my first question was, "Will I be able to walk again?"

My mum dropped off an overnight bag but she wasn't allowed to come and see me because the pandemic was very much in full swing and the hospital had a strict zero visitor policy. The only way she'd be able to see me was if she engineered it so she also broke a bone but I thought that was a bit of a stretch.

I arrived at my ward shortly after 3.30am feeling incredibly overwhelmed and disheartened, wanting nothing but a hug from my mum.

To recap: I now had no front tooth and a broken ankle. And I needed an operation.

SEVEN

My grandma, Margaret, died on 22nd June 2020. She had dementia and a minor heart condition so her death didn't come as much of a surprise, but it was yet another tragic event to add to the list of Lucy's Tragic Events: 2020 Edition.

For the last month of her life, my grandma lived in hospital. She had her own room and twenty-four hour care, and most of her time was spent asleep, dosed up on morphine. Visiting was restricted due to the pandemic, but when we could go and see her we made sure to hold her hand and tell her we loved her.

Having her own room made it incredibly lonely, and looking around at the drab walls and box window, I felt disheartened and depressed. Looking at my grandma, near the end of her life, I knew this would be me one day. It was a mini wake up call, when you're faced with the prospect of death and nothing else seems particularly important.

Hospital isn't an exciting place under normal circumstances but during a pandemic, it's dark and quiet and cold. Where there would normally be the bustle of visitors, or the rush of staff attending patients, there were empty corridors and silence.

We were allowed into the ward one at a time, and we had to wear masks, gloves and a plastic apron. As we came away into the car park, I felt grateful that I could come away and that I wasn't stuck in there like a prisoner. I was free to do whatever I wanted.

Wrong! This is 2020, remember?

Following 'the incident' at the skate park, I was an inpatient for twenty-three days. Prior to this, I'd never spent any significant time in hospital other than when I was born and luckily for us, a baby's memory is shite.

How did you cope, you ask? HA. HA. HA. HA. Good one. The morning after 'the incident': there was a drip in my arm pumping painkillers through my body and I was wearing a chic pink nighty that had no back. My toes looked pathetic poking out the top of my cast, which was balanced precariously on three pillows. I'd had three hours sleep.

I was in a room with four other women and one of them had just gotten out of bed, dressed and walked out in a huff. I don't know why but if it was about the food she could've done more, in my opinion. Overturned a bed or something.

Another lady had a broken knee from being hit by a taxi outside her place of work, which coincidentally happened to be the hospital we were in. If you're going to get hit by a car anywhere, outside a hospital is probably quite good, I suppose. I didn't say that though.

Because of the pandemic, each bed was so far apart we might as well have been at the Grand Canyon. It was impossible to start any kind of conversation with my new neighbours, so I didn't.

Charlotte delivered a bag of goodies, which included chocolate and a couple of books. I opened *What A Time To Be Alone* by Chidera Eggerue and waited for news about my ankle.

EIGHT

Before all of this shite I was extremely squeamish when it came to broken bones. We all have that thing that makes our eyes go fuzzy and our chest feel tight, and my thing was bones.

When my sister broke her ankle in 2012, I had to hold myself up on the side of her bed when the doctor was talking because I wanted to collapse. When I was eleven, my friend Anousheh invited me to the cinema to watch Million Dollar Baby for her birthday. If you've never seen Million Dollar Baby, Hilary Swank is a really hench amateur boxer who gets her nose broken half way through the film. How does the film end? I wouldn't know because I was in the toilet with Anousheh's mum with my head under the dryer.

The eventuality that I would one day break a bone of my own was something I'd always dreaded. I hated thinking about broken bones in other people's bodies, but in my own body? I was sure I'd just shrivel into a raisin and die.

In A&E, the night of 'the incident', I was given a vape full of morphine, which I was told to suck on a few times before the doctor rearranged my bones. He lifted my foot, pushed it backwards, tugged it forwards, massaged it until he was satisfied my breaks and fractures were in some kind of uniform. My emotions, however, were in tatters. I'm not joking when I say I cried out in pain like a little boy getting kicked in the bollocks.

The nurse, who had bowed her head during the procedure as if she understood my agony, then plastered up my leg in a cast. When she had finished, the floor was white as though someone had spilled an entire bottle of talcum powder. My face was the same colour.

The following day, a nurse brought me lunch, which was a microwavable curry and a bowl of soup. I know everyone says hospital food is shite but take it from me, hospital food is shite. If you saw me once I'd been discharged and I looked like Gollum, apologies. This is why.

Soon I was wheeled to my new ward where I would stay until my operation date. During lockdown, there had been an increase in skateboarding injuries, the porter told me.

"The girl who was in the bed before you also broke her ankle skateboarding."

I smiled to be polite but I was in no mood to hold a conversation. The people pleaser in me felt like an arse but my foot wasn't attached to my leg so I felt like I had an excuse.

My new room for the foreseeable future. Margaret across the way was eighty-eight years old and had the sweetest smile I'd ever seen. She'd broken her hip the month before and spent extra time in hospital after contracting pneumonia.

In the bed next to her was Joan, eighty-five years old. She'd had pioneering surgery on her leg during the summer, which meant she wasn't able to walk unaided, and was the longest-serving resident of the ward by far, having been there over two hundred days.

Next-door to me was Debbie, a middle-aged woman going through the menopause who had fallen down a hole in her garden chasing her cat. She was loud and had the strangest metal scaffolding sticking out of her ankle holding her shattered bones together.

Working on three hours sleep, I really didn't want to talk to anyone. I was nervous about the idea of having my first major operation and I still hadn't seen my family following 'the incident' at the skate park.

Despite being surrounded by people, I felt desperately alone. So instead of engaging in conversation, I sunk into my armchair and opened my book.

The following day, I was introduced to my new friend, oxycodone, an incredibly strong opiate painkiller. It came in two forms: a slow release tablet, which I took every twelve hours, and a fast acting liquid shot, which I took every four. I've since read that when taken orally it has about 1.5 times the effects of morphine. So you can imagine it was strong. I was high off my titty tits. Use my blood pressure armband as a hat? Why not! Draw a blue moustache and goatee on my face? Sure! Stick my foam ear plugs in my nostrils and take my denture out? Absolutely! Any dignity I'd had prior to 'the incident' disappeared the moment I was wheeled into that room. But my god, did we laugh.

Margaret wasn't allowed to eat because of her pneumonia so as I ate my lunch of a cheese sandwich and crisps, I tried my best not to make eye contact with her. I thought that was fair.

There were obvious similarities between Margaret and my grandma other than the same name and the grey perm. Margaret was eighty-eight (my grandma was eighty-nine) and - well, that's about it really. What more do you want from me? But with some lingering grief from the death of my grandma, I was drawn to her.

Often we would sit together, hand in hand, and she'd tell me about her life in Manchester. We'd talk about Coronation Street and her favourite food (fish and chips). She told me about her dog who she loved dearly but who had passed away recently. I showed her pictures of my cat, Beans.

One day Margaret was feeling down because she couldn't eat anything (they fed her through a drip), so while she was asleep I drew a picture of her and stuck it to the table so she'd see it when she woke up. The four of us were basically strangers but we had the shared experience of living with each other twenty-four hours a day, seven days a week.

My time in hospital turned out to be a massive jolly. The Sister said it was OK for me to have my guitar on the ward and I spent several nights singing Elvis and The Beatles with my new pals. Some of the nurses came in and sang along with us, dancing when they should've been working. We were in our own bubble and we knew nothing of the outside world. I didn't watch TV or listen to music when I was in hospital; I didn't need to. There was twenty-four hour entertainment around us at all times.

My section of the ward looked like my bedroom at home. I kept my cursed skateboard on the window sill as a reminder, along with a pile of books, snacks, drinks, a yo-yo, colouring pencils and a bag of clothes.

I received a lot of gifts from friends and family, which was nice. One of my mates even offered to smuggle in wood-fired pizza for me.

Because of coronavirus, visiting was restricted, which meant I only saw one member of my family for thirty minutes every few days. I was lonely and missed everyone important in my life but I knew I had to make the best of the situation if I was going to survive.

Carlos, the hospital's morale officer, brought us art supplies and games and books. I made a bridge out of paper straws strong enough to hold a jug of water and won an ice-cream. I learnt how to make balloon animals and origami flowers. I forced my roommates to play a game of Shag, Marry, Kill and it went down better than anticipated. Debbie is moist for Richard Gere, it turns out.

By day ten, Joan, Debbie, Margaret and I were basically family, taking the piss, farting in front of each other, and laughing most nights before bed.

Just shy of two weeks after I'd arrived in hospital, a nurse came in and told us Margaret would be moving to a ward that could offer her better care. A couple of days later, Margaret passed away. I cried so much a nurse brought me a cup of tea and a biscuit.

I'll never forget the moment Margaret left our ward, clutching the paper flower I'd made her. She looked at me and said, "No more skateboarding."

I spent just under two weeks with Margaret but I loved her dearly with all of my heart.

NINE

Emotions were rampant by day fourteen and I still hadn't had my operation.

The Covid-19 pandemic meant longer preparation time, which meant fewer operations per day, which in turn meant a longer waiting list. Plus factor in the surge of dopes trying skateboarding for the first time and breaking bits of their body. Fuckin' idiots.

It started to feel a bit like Groundhog Day the longer I spent in hospital. We had the same routine every day: breakfast at 8am; crying at 9am; lunch at 12pm; tea at 5pm; blood pressure and temperature checks at 10am, 2pm, 6pm, 10pm, 2am and 6am. For someone who'd spent the summer waking up after ten on most days, it was all a bit regimented for my liking.

If there was ever a day that you wanted alone time, haha! Think again. The only time you could have a break was in the bathroom. Sometimes I'd hide in there and pretend I was doing a really big poo just to give my energy levels a chance to replenish. Other times I'd pretend to have a nap in the middle of the day. A lot of the time I actually had a nap in the middle of the day. I'm sociable at the best of times but fuck me, I was exhausted.

Not every day was easy, either. By this point, Debbie, Joan and I were so close that we openly cried in front of each other whenever we felt shit. I've dealt with periods of anxiety and depression for most of my life, and being stuck in the same place day after day often intensified those feelings.

Hopelessness lingered in our room for a few days. Debbie and I took it in turns to cry while Joan tried to make us laugh. I couldn't imagine being in her position, spending nearly a year in the same hospital room without seeing her family.

I was offered a support session from a hospital psychologist and I accepted. He told me everything I was feeling was valid and normal given the circumstances, and he was absolutely right. Physically, I was healing but mentally, I was struggling.

On day eighteen I got the news that I'd be having my operation. Three weeks away from home, my bed, my comforts, my pet, my family, with my leg in a cast and shite food. One day I was offered a jacket potato with a side of mash. I politely declined.

I'd never had an operation before and I was terrified. I was convinced I'd be put under and never wake up. Despite what everyone was telling me, medical professionals included, I was sure they were all wrong and this was the end.

I texted a few friends to say I loved them and that I was thankful they'd always been there for me. I had the preliminary tests, signed the consent forms and put on my little cotton knickers. I was also on my period and a nurse gave me a pad the size of a slice of bread to stick inside the little cotton knickers.

I felt sick to my stomach and my mouth had about as much moisture as a sandpaper sandwich. A doctor told me my bones were already three weeks healed and therefore would need re-breaking during surgery. So that was fun.

Whenever I'd imagined having an operation I'd pictured scenes from films with those alien-looking light circles on the ceiling, and it turns out it is exactly like that. Kudos to film researchers.

It was time to be put under and the anaesthetist pumped some thick white liquid into my hand. There was a tingling sensation in my head and then I woke up three hours later in the recovery room. It was that easy. (It was that easy for me. I'm sure for the surgeon it was at least a bit challenging).

Instead of a cast, I had one of those futuristic looking grey boots that astronauts probably don't wear. It had two buttons on the front: a big one to pump air into the boot and a small one to deflate it.

They'd sliced my lower leg on both sides and inserted two screws and a metal plate, which I was told would hold my re-broken bones in place. I was wheeled back to my room so groggy I didn't have a fucking clue what day it was. But after three weeks in hospital, I was finally fixed.

Three days later, it was time for me to leave. I'm not kidding when I say you could've dragged me out of there kicking and screaming. After three and a half weeks of routine, socialisation, laughter, drugs and creativity, I was due to return to normality. And I didn't want to.

Debbie went home after a successful operation and a grey space boot just like mine. Joan asked for my number and wrote it in her black book. The day before I was due to leave, she got the news that she would be transferred to a hospital in Lancashire closer to home, where they would help her learn to walk again. Just before she left, we held hands and cried.

TEN

Sitting at home in bed with my boot propped up and a cup of tea, I had another cry. Hospital had been my home for so long that it was incredibly depressing to be faced with silence and solitude.

A lot of the people I'd bonded with, I wouldn't see again. Somebody I'd cared for and loved, even for a short time, had passed away. I couldn't walk and I didn't have much strength to use my crutches. Suddenly, I was faced with reality after weeks of living in a bubble. And I hated it.

If I could go back to the moment I broke my ankle and prevent it, I wouldn't. Being in hospital changed my life in so many ways and even still, I am immensely grateful for that experience.

Despite the ups and downs, there was a great sense of community and family amongst staff and patients. It was a chance to reset some of the bad habits I'd fallen into at the beginning of the year and start fresh. I'd watched somebody see out the end of their life and it made me incredibly grateful that I am at the start of mine. I don't want to be on my death bed regretting things I should've done but didn't because I was nervous, or tired, or worried about what people thought.

So take this as a sign: do whatever it is you're putting off because you're a bit scared. And if it doesn't work out, at least you tried.

ELEVEN

A few days after my boot came off, I tested positive for Covid-19.

Rewind to six weeks earlier: it was mid-September and by this point, I was mentally and physically exhausted. Because of the global pandemic, I wasn't worried about missing much while my ankle was healing. Most of my mates were following the rules and isolating, and bars and pubs had a strict 10pm curfew. So for six weeks, I let my ankle do its thing.

Things to consider while recovering from a broken ankle:

1) You must shower sitting down.

2) You must wear a plastic bag over your boot in the shower.

3) When you take the boot off, it stinks.

4) You have the option of going up the stairs on your bum.

5) If you make a cup of tea, don't even think about carrying it anywhere.

6) If you're stubborn and decide to make a cup of tea and you inevitably spill it, you'll need a family member to mop it up.

7) Your pets will be scared of the boot.

8) Your pets will be scared of your crutches.

9) Your pets will be scared of the smell coming out of your boot.

10) Eventually, showering and getting out of bed doesn't seem that important.

11) You will nap a lot.

During my recovery, I spent so many days in bed, asleep. I would sleep for twelve hours a night, wake up, eat something and then go back upstairs to sleep. This was becoming my new routine and I started to feel guilty for not working hard enough to get my life back on track. I was furloughed from my job and faced days of doing nothing. Why wasn't I being more productive? The simple answer is, I was healing.

Rest is important for our mental and physical health and we shouldn't be ashamed to admit when we need a break. I didn't feel control in certain aspects of my life but I knew I could be in control of my health.

And it's OK to feel like you've not got your shit together. Let's get this out of the way: no-one has their shit together. Even the people who seem like they do.

There's nothing worse than comparing yourself to other people and their timelines. No two people are the same, so why are we so obsessed with following what others are doing?

I used to compare myself to others and what they were achieving, feeling as though I was achieving nothing. It was an incredible waste of time. Use that energy for something more productive like writing a book or shaving your legs. (If that's your thing. Today I shaved half of my leg and then realised I didn't care).

Celebrate the small wins, in whatever form they come. Getting out of bed, having a shower and changing your clothes feels like winning when you're healing, whether it's mentally or physically.

I took my first steps without my crutches after ten weeks and it felt like winning the lottery. Walking was alien but at least I was moving. Two days later, I tested positive for Covid-19.

Suddenly, I was back to square one.

TWELVE

Having Covid-19 didn't feel anything like I thought it would. But then again, neither did breaking my ankle or losing my front tooth.

I am fortunate enough to say I was one of the lucky ones. The worst symptom I had was a blocked nose, and then a few days later I lost my taste and smell.

Ten days isolation gave me time to organise my thoughts and reflect on a year full of abnormally unlucky events. But these unfortunate experiences weren't for nothing, I realised.

I've been lucky enough to grow and learn and build up strength ready for future hardships I know I'm going to face. Now if I have bad days, I'm confident that they will pass. I'll sit with my feelings, acknowledge them, vent to my best friend Vic, and then move on.

No feeling is permanent, whether it's positive or negative, physical or mental.

As I'm writing this, I'm sitting in bed with my legs crossed. I can feel the metal plates attached to my bones, causing a dull ache. I'm exhausted and I'm not eating enough. There are dark circles under my eyes and my nail varnish is chipped. I haven't seen my fringe for weeks. My ankle has healed and I'm walking again. I recovered from Covid-19 without passing it onto my family.

I have an appointment booked for a brace, which will straighten a few crooked teeth. An appointment I probably wouldn't have booked if I hadn't lost my front tooth. Then I will have my permanent implant fitted. These are things that I'm looking forward to but they aren't things that will define my happiness.

I have found ways of being content despite these imperfections. Having a missing front tooth is just something I live with and I laugh about. I know it's not forever but even if it was, it wouldn't be the end of the world. After all, the birth of One Tooth Luce is a funny story to tell. It's something I can talk about on first dates, or with my children, or when I start a new job.

This may not seem like a lot to accept but for me, this is huge. The weightlessness attached to not caring is extremely powerful and strengthening.

I spent years as a teenager hiding from bullies who picked on me for the way I looked. I hated my body when I should've been thanking it every day for keeping me alive. I don't love everything about myself but now, those hang-ups are not as important. Worse things have happened and worse things will happen than me hating on my double chin or my squishy belly or my missing tooth.

What has this year taught us? It has taught me that I'm terrible at action sports and that I should stay away from concerts involving male siblings.

Breaking a bone isn't as scary as I'd once imagined. Creating a persona for your missing front tooth will most likely make your friends laugh. People will fancy you despite your imperfections. Perfection is boring and unrealistic.

If you're eating hummus, try not to spill it down the crack of your space boot. Something significant, like losing a family member or a global pandemic, can come along and remind us not to take some of the smaller things for granted.

I've realised how loved I am and how much I can love myself. We need to love ourselves because there's nobody else out there like us. I would bet all of my possessions that there isn't another One Tooth Luce out there. If there is and you're reading this, come to Manchester and I'll buy you a pint.

If this pandemic has taught us anything, it's that what we really, really want to do is what we should be doing. This year and its set of unfortunate events has given me a chance to re-evaluate what I want from life and explore other opportunities I may not have been brave enough to try before.

Amongst all of the terrible things that have happened, there has been a lot of good. I've launched a photography zine, I've photographed some of my favourite bands and singers, I've been interviewed for a magazine, and I've met some of the most incredible people who have shaped my 2020. And I've written this book.

A few things before I go. There is never a right time for anything and if you haven't done it yet, go and do it. Who knows how long we'll be here for. You will have fun, you will make mistakes and you will piss people off but everything is temporary. In a hundred years, no-one will have known you existed. Try not to worry too much.

xoxo One Tooth Luce

ABOUT THE AUTHOR

Luce studied for an MA in Creating Writing at the Manchester Writing School. She enjoys freaking people out by removing her denture. She's also never touching a skateboard again.

Printed in Great Britain
by Amazon